Building a Legacy: A Guide to Creating Financial Security for Future Generations

Welcome to "Building a Legacy," an eBook designed to help you create a financial legacy that will benefit your children and future generations. In this comprehensive guide, we'll explore practical strategies, insightful tips, and actionable advice to empower you to build wealth, instill financial values, and lay the groundwork for a secure financial future for your family. Whether you're just starting your journey to financial independence or looking to enhance your existing wealth-building strategies, this eBook will provide you with the tools and knowledge you need to leave a lasting legacy for your loved ones.

Chapter 1: Understanding Generational Wealth

- Defining Generational Wealth: Explore the concept of generational wealth and its significance in securing your family's financial future. Learn how generational wealth extends beyond monetary assets to include values, knowledge, and opportunities passed down through generations.

- The Benefits of Generational Wealth: Understand the advantages of building generational wealth, including providing financial security, creating opportunities, and fostering a sense of legacy and identity for future descendants.

- Breaking the Cycle of Financial Instability: Recognize the importance of breaking the cycle of financial instability and creating a foundation of financial security for your family. Understand how generational wealth can empower future generations to pursue their dreams and achieve their fullest potential.

Chapter 2: Building Wealth for Future Generations

- Setting Financial Goals: Identify your family's financial goals and aspirations, both short-term and long-term. Explore strategies for setting SMART (Specific, Measurable, Achievable, Relevant, Time-bound) goals that align with your values and priorities.

- Creating a Wealth-Building Plan: Develop a customized wealth-building plan that incorporates saving, investing, and strategic financial management techniques. Learn how to maximize your earning potential, minimize expenses, and grow your wealth over time.

- Diversifying Your Assets: Explore the importance of diversification in building generational wealth. Learn how to invest in a variety of asset classes, including stocks, bonds, real estate, and alternative investments, to reduce risk and maximize returns.

Chapter 3: Instilling Financial Values in Your Children

- Teaching Financial Literacy: Recognize the importance of teaching your children about money management, saving, and investing from a young age. Explore age-appropriate strategies for introducing financial concepts and fostering healthy money habits.

- Leading by Example: Understand the powerful influence of parental behavior on children's financial attitudes and behaviors. Learn how to model positive financial behaviors and values in your own life, including responsible spending, saving, and charitable giving.

- Encouraging Entrepreneurship and Innovation: Explore ways to encourage your children to develop an entrepreneurial mindset and pursue opportunities for innovation and creativity. Teach them about the value of hard work, perseverance, and resilience in achieving financial success.

Chapter 4: Estate Planning and Wealth Transfer

- Creating a Comprehensive Estate Plan: Understand the importance of estate planning in preserving and transferring your wealth to future generations. Learn about essential estate planning documents, including wills, trusts, powers of attorney, and advanced healthcare directives.

- Minimizing Taxes and Probate Costs: Explore strategies for minimizing estate taxes and probate costs to maximize the value of your estate for your heirs. Learn about tax-efficient estate planning techniques, such as gifting, charitable giving, and trust planning.

- Educating Heirs and Successors: Prepare your heirs and successors to inherit and manage their inheritance responsibly. Provide ongoing financial education, support, and guidance to empower them to make informed decisions and preserve and grow the family's wealth.

Chapter 5: Leaving a Legacy of Generosity and Impact

- Philanthropy and Charitable Giving: Explore the role of philanthropy and charitable giving in leaving a legacy of generosity and impact. Learn how to incorporate charitable giving into your estate plan and involve your family in philanthropic activities.

- Creating a Family Mission Statement: Develop a family mission statement that reflects your shared values, goals, and aspirations for the future. Use your mission statement as a guide for making financial decisions and prioritizing activities that align with your family's legacy.

- Making a Difference in the World: Inspire your family to make a difference in the world by leveraging their wealth, talents, and resources to address pressing social, environmental, and humanitarian challenges. Encourage them to become agents of positive change and leave a lasting impact on future generations.

Chapter 6: Ensuring Continuity and Sustainability

- Establishing Family Governance Structures

- Educating Future Generations

- Implementing Wealth Preservation Strategies

- Fostering a Culture of Stewardship

Table of Contents

Chapter 1 9

Chapter 2... 11

Chapter 3... 13

Chapter 4... 15

Chapter 5... 17

Chapter 6... 19

Chapter 1

Understanding Generational Wealth

Generational wealth is more than just a sum of money passed down from one generation to the next; it encompasses a legacy of financial stability, opportunities, and values that endure over time. In this chapter, we'll delve into the concept of generational wealth and explore its significance in shaping the future of your family.

1. Defining Generational Wealth:

Generational wealth refers to the accumulation of assets, resources, and knowledge passed down through generations within a family. It includes financial assets such as money, investments, and property, as well as non-financial assets such as education, skills, and values.

2. The Benefits of Generational Wealth:

- Financial Security: Generational wealth provides a safety net for future generations, ensuring they have the resources they need to weather financial challenges and pursue their goals.

- Opportunities for Success: With generational wealth comes access to educational opportunities, career advancement, and entrepreneurial ventures that can propel future generations to success.

- Sense of Legacy and Identity: Generational wealth fosters a sense of identity and belonging within a family, as heirs inherit not only financial assets but also the values, traditions, and stories of those who came before them.

3. Breaking the Cycle of Financial Instability:

For many families, generational wealth represents a break from the cycle of financial instability and hardship that may have characterized previous generations. By prioritizing financial literacy, responsible money management, and strategic wealth-building, you can lay the foundation for a brighter financial future for your children and grandchildren.

Understanding generational wealth is the first step toward building a lasting legacy for your family. By recognizing the value of financial stability, opportunities, and values passed down through generations, you can set the stage for a prosperous future for your loved ones.

Chapter 2

Building a Solid Financial Foundation for Future Generations

In this chapter, we'll explore practical strategies and actionable steps to help you build a solid financial foundation that will benefit your children and future generations.

1. Setting Financial Goals:

- Start by defining your family's financial goals, both short-term and long-term. Consider factors such as education, homeownership, retirement, and philanthropy.

- Use the SMART (Specific, Measurable, Achievable, Relevant, Time-bound) criteria to ensure your goals are clear and actionable. For example, instead of saying "save for retirement," specify an amount and timeframe, such as "save $1 million for retirement by age 65."

2. Creating a Wealth-Building Plan:

- Develop a comprehensive wealth-building plan that outlines how you will achieve your financial goals. Consider factors such as income, expenses, savings, investments, and debt management.

- Break down your goals into smaller, manageable steps and create a timeline for achieving each milestone. Monitor your progress regularly and make adjustments as needed to stay on track.

3. Diversifying Your Assets:

- Diversification is key to building a resilient financial portfolio that can withstand market fluctuations and economic downturns. Spread your investments across different asset classes, industries, and geographic regions to minimize risk.

- Consider investing in a mix of stocks, bonds, real estate, and alternative investments such as commodities, cryptocurrencies, or precious metals. Consult with a financial advisor to develop a diversified investment strategy tailored to your risk tolerance and financial goals.

By setting clear financial goals, creating a strategic wealth-building plan, and diversifying your assets, you can lay a solid financial foundation that will benefit your children and future generations for years to come.

Chapter 3

Instilling Financial Values in Your Children

Empowering your children with financial knowledge and instilling positive money habits early in life is essential for their long-term financial well-being. In this chapter, we'll explore practical strategies for teaching your children about money management and fostering a healthy relationship with finances.

1. Teaching Financial Literacy:

- Start by introducing basic financial concepts to your children in age-appropriate ways. Use every day experiences, such as shopping trips or allowance discussions, as opportunities to teach them about topics like budgeting, saving, and spending.

- Utilize educational resources such as books, games, and online videos to make financial learning fun and engaging for your children. Look for materials that are tailored to their age group and learning style.

2. Leading by Example:

- Children learn by example, so it's essential to model positive financial behaviors and attitudes in your own life. Demonstrate responsible money management practices such as budgeting, saving for goals, and avoiding impulse purchases.

- Involve your children in family financial discussions and decisions whenever possible. Encourage them to ask questions and share their thoughts and opinions on money matters.

3. Encouraging Entrepreneurship and Innovation:

- Foster an entrepreneurial mindset in your children by encouraging them to explore their interests, develop creative solutions to problems, and take calculated risks. Support their entrepreneurial endeavors by providing guidance, resources, and encouragement.

- Help your children identify opportunities to earn money through activities such as starting a small business, freelancing, or participating in community events. Encourage them to save and invest a portion of their earnings to develop good financial habits from a young age.

By teaching your children about financial literacy, leading by example, and encouraging entrepreneurship and innovation, you can empower them to make smart financial decisions and build a strong foundation for their financial future.

Chapter 4

Estate Planning and Wealth Transfer

Effective estate planning is crucial for ensuring that your wealth is transferred to your children and future generations in accordance with your wishes. In this chapter, we'll explore the key components of estate planning and strategies for minimizing taxes and probate costs.

1. Creating a Comprehensive Estate Plan:

- Begin by inventorying your assets, including bank accounts, investments, real estate, business interests, and personal belongings. Identify beneficiaries for each asset and consider how you would like your estate to be distributed.

- Work with an estate planning attorney to draft essential documents, such as wills, trusts, powers of attorney, and advanced healthcare directives. These documents will outline your wishes regarding asset distribution, guardianship of minor children, and healthcare decisions in the event of incapacity.

2. Minimizing Taxes and Probate Costs:

- Explore strategies for minimizing estate taxes and probate costs to preserve the value of your estate for your heirs. Consider utilizing trusts, lifetime gifts, and charitable giving to reduce the tax burden on your estate.

- Review beneficiary designations on retirement accounts, life insurance policies, and other assets to ensure they are up to date and aligned with your estate plan. Naming beneficiaries directly can help these assets avoid probate and pass directly to your heirs.

3. Educating Heirs and Successors:

- Prepare your heirs and successors to inherit and manage their inheritance responsibly. Provide them with ongoing financial education, support, and guidance to ensure they understand their rights and responsibilities.

- Consider involving your heirs in family meetings or discussions about wealth transfer and estate planning. Encourage open communication and transparency to help them feel prepared and empowered to handle their financial legacy.

By creating a comprehensive estate plan, minimizing taxes and probate costs, and educating your heirs and successors, you can ensure that your wealth is transferred to future generations smoothly and efficiently. Effective estate planning allows you to leave a lasting legacy for your children and future descendants while preserving your family's financial security and prosperity.

Chapter 5

Leaving a Legacy of Generosity and Impact

In this final chapter, we'll explore the importance of leaving a legacy of generosity and impact for your children and future generations. By incorporating philanthropy, values-based decision-making, and a focus on making a positive difference in the world, you can create a lasting legacy that extends far beyond financial wealth.

1. Philanthropy and Charitable Giving:

- Explore the role of philanthropy and charitable giving in leaving a legacy of generosity and impact. Consider causes and organizations that align with your family's values and priorities, such as education, healthcare, environmental conservation, or social justice.

- Involve your children in philanthropic activities and decision-making processes. Encourage them to research and select charitable organizations to support and participate in volunteering or fundraising efforts.

2. Creating a Family Mission Statement:

- Develop a family mission statement that reflects your shared values, goals, and aspirations for the future. Use this mission statement as a guide for making financial decisions, prioritizing activities, and aligning your actions with your family's legacy.

- Discuss the importance of giving back to your community and making a positive impact in the world. Encourage your children to consider how they can use their talents, resources, and privileges to help others and create positive change.

3. Making a Difference in the World:

- Inspire your family to make a difference in the world by leveraging their wealth, influence, and expertise to address pressing social, environmental, and humanitarian challenges. Encourage them to become active participants in creating positive change and leaving a lasting impact on future generations.

- Lead by example by participating in philanthropic initiatives, volunteering your time and skills, and advocating for causes that are important to your family. Emphasize the importance of empathy, compassion, and social responsibility in shaping your family's legacy.

By incorporating philanthropy, values-based decision-making, and a focus on making a positive difference in the world, you can leave a legacy that extends far beyond financial wealth. By instilling these values in your children and future generations, you empower them to become agents of positive change and create a brighter, more compassionate world for generations to come.

Chapter 6

Ensuring Continuity and Sustainability

In this chapter, we'll explore strategies for ensuring the continuity and sustainability of your family's financial legacy across multiple generations. By implementing proactive measures and fostering a culture of stewardship, you can preserve and grow your wealth for the benefit of future descendants.

1. Establishing Family Governance Structures:

- Consider establishing family governance structures, such as a family council or advisory board, to facilitate communication, decision-making, and conflict resolution among family members. These structures can help promote unity, transparency, and shared responsibility for managing the family's wealth.

- Define roles and responsibilities within the family governance framework, including the selection of family leaders, decision-making processes, and mechanisms for addressing disputes or disagreements. Encourage active participation and engagement from all family members to ensure the success of the governance system.

2. Educating Future Generations:

- Invest in the education and development of future generations to ensure they have the knowledge, skills, and values needed to manage and grow the family's wealth responsibly. Provide opportunities for financial literacy training, leadership development, and mentorship within the family.

- Create formalized programs or initiatives to educate heirs and successors about the family's history, values, and wealth management principles. Encourage experiential learning opportunities, such as internships, apprenticeships, or participation in family business ventures, to help future leaders gain practical experience and perspective.

3. Implementing Wealth Preservation Strategies:

- Develop a comprehensive wealth preservation plan that includes strategies for protecting and growing the family's assets over time. Consider factors such as asset protection, tax optimization, risk management, and succession planning.

- Work with a team of trusted advisors, including financial planners, attorneys, accountants, and investment professionals, to implement wealth preservation strategies tailored to your family's needs and goals. Regularly review and update your plan to adapt to changing circumstances and market conditions.

4. Fostering a Culture of Stewardship:

- Instill a culture of stewardship within your family that emphasizes responsible management, ethical conduct, and long-term thinking. Encourage a sense of ownership and accountability among family members for safeguarding and enhancing the family's wealth for future generations.

- Lead by example by demonstrating integrity, humility, and a commitment to serving others. Encourage open dialogue and collaboration among family members to foster trust, respect, and unity in stewarding the family's financial legacy.

By establishing family governance structures, educating future generations, implementing wealth preservation strategies, and fostering a culture of stewardship, you can ensure the continuity and sustainability of your family's financial legacy for generations to come. By taking proactive measures to preserve and grow your wealth, you empower your family to thrive and prosper long into the future.

In "Building a Lasting Legacy: A Guide to Creating Financial Security for Future Generations," we've explored the essential elements of creating a financial legacy that extends far beyond monetary wealth. From understanding the concept of generational wealth to instilling financial values in your children, from effective estate planning to leaving a legacy of generosity and impact, each chapter has offered insights, strategies, and practical tips to help you build a legacy that lasts.

As you reflect on the journey we've taken together, remember that building a lasting legacy is not just about accumulating wealth; it's about investing in the well-being and prosperity of your family and future generations. By prioritizing financial education, instilling positive values, and fostering a culture of stewardship, you can empower your children and descendants to navigate life's challenges and seize opportunities with confidence and resilience.

As you embark on this journey, keep in mind that creating a financial legacy is an ongoing process that requires dedication, commitment, and adaptability. Stay open to new ideas, be willing to embrace change, and always strive to lead by example in your financial decisions and actions. By doing so, you can build a legacy that enriches the lives of your loved ones and leaves a lasting impact on the world.

Thank you for joining me on this journey to build a lasting legacy for future generations. May your efforts be guided by wisdom, compassion, and a vision for a brighter future for all.

L JC

www.ingramcontent.com/pod-product-compliance
Lightning Source LLC
Chambersburg PA
CBHW071001220526
45471CB00007B/3134